AMERICA
SEES A HUE

For Those Who Pretend
Not to Understand Cancel Culture

MONICA R. WRIGHT

To order additional copies of this book, contact:
Xlibris
844-714-8691
www.Xlibris.com
Orders@Xlibris.com

ISBN: Softcover   978-1-6698-0189-4
         EBook   978-1-6698-0188-7

Print information available on the last page

Rev. date: 02/02/2022

Once upon a time in the land of the free, not everyone was free like we were supposed to be.

Once I explain our sorted history, you will understand the need to change our country.

When our country was founded a long time ago, imagine the people were the colors of a rainbow.

Red was here first, this was their native land, white came along with a different plan.

Red was very kind to the people of no hue. They fed them a feast and taught them everything they knew.

But instead of being grateful to their new red friends, the people of no hue put them on reservations.

The kind and gentle natives had been overthrown, as the people of no hue claimed the land as their own.

In order to justify how they pillaged and ravaged, they told everyone that the red people were savages.

They buried many of the kind red people in graves, then headed to Africa to buy black people to enslave.

The people they purchased were kings and queens, they were intelligent and hard-working adults and teens.

They packed them tightly in the bottom of ships and did this repeatedly, they made several trips.

The voyage was long and brutal, and many wouldn't survive, but not as long and brutal as the rest of their lives.

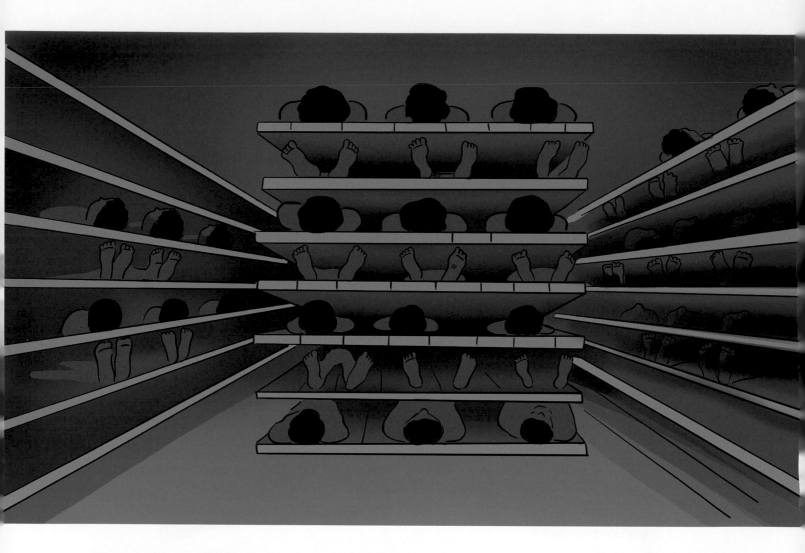

They were stripped of their clothes, names and even their God and sold like property and worked very hard.

They took children from mothers and husbands from wives and beat them and worked them for the rest for their lives.

They even replaced their names and gave them their own, as they reaped untold fortunes from the crops that were grown.

The slaves received nothing for all of their labor, they were property and often sold to their neighbors.

They weren't allowed to read, were forced to breed and meet any and all of a white person's needs.

The people of no hue used the blood sweat and tears of the black people to build fortunes for four hundred years.

But then some of the white people who were not vicious or cruel thought the practice of slavery was totally uncool.

The white people that thought slavery should end, went to war with the ones who refused to bend.

Finally, one day black people were free, but no thanks to a cruel confederacy.

They fought tooth and nail to keep the black people in chains because they couldn't survive without them because they didn't have the brains.

Even though slavery ended a long time ago, black people were still subjected to things like Jim Crow.

Black people tried to build their own towns, but bad white people would come along and burn it all down.

They terrorized black people and hung them from trees but never served jail time for these atrocities.

There were places black people couldn't go and things they couldn't do, to justify this, white people shaped your view.

They told you black men were criminals in movies and on tv, and black women were maids and whores and mammies.

They did the same to the red people and yellow people too, they only wanted you to respect the people of no hue.

This went on for years because there was a bigger fight, the black people were focused on the fight for civil rights.

And women were fighting for their rights too, and all women not just the women of no hue.

Now that most of the battles have been fought and won, we want our country to represent everyone.

There were monuments, and statues made from plaster and buildings and streets named after slave masters.

All intended to honor these men, who died for the enslavement of other Americans.

Movies, songs, tv shows and cartoons that were made to make black people look like buffoons.

Native Americans as mascots and Asians as logos, reminders of how things were long ago. Americans know that in order to grow, all of these hateful images had to go.

So the people with hues, along with the Jews, joined with a party that called itself blue.

Team blue knew what we had to do for people of color, Jews and the LGBTQ.

The blue team sought to help those in need and to make things fair so we could all succeed.

Although the cruel people of no hue were not the majority but only a few, they organized online to form a group for them too, and together they decided to call their group Q.

Q was comprised of unintelligent guys and grew in size by spreading strange lies.

They preyed on the fears of their colorless peers and were lead by an orange man who lived for their cheers. His hateful speeches were music to their ears and fodder for many political careers.

No one could deny that he repeatedly lied, and committed crimes they couldn't justify but they tried and tried, some willing to die, because the Orangeman offered them pie in the sky.

The man with orange skin promised if he wins that he would make America great again.

The rest of the colors knew that by "again" he meant way back when it was ruled by white men.

So to distract the colors from his failings and scandals, they developed a phrase called the culture of cancel.

They made fun of the blue teams fight for inclusion by spreading more lies and causing confusion.

The orange man held rallies spreading lies and fear and won the election and ruled for four years.

The countries new President was incompetent and obscene, and his colleagues were too cowardly and weak to intervene. Telling lies was a regular routine, on twitter, FOX news and by any means.

He was the worst leader the country had ever seen. He even lied about a virus causing a year of quarantine so bad to survive the country needed a vaccine, all caused by a man who was the color of a tangerine.

So many black people were killed by the police, the good people marched for justice and peace.

Tired of being oppressed, they marched in protest and to beg law enforcement to at least make an arrest.

But the new president simply had no interest, in obliging the good people's simple request so he sent soldiers with weapons and bullet proof vests to deal with the good people's civil unrest

He lied so much that when he lost the election, his brainwashed followers committed an insurrection.

Now they claim they want unity because they lost at the polls, and the Orangeman and turtle was no longer in control.

The blue people rule because they won fair and square and the past year had been a pandemic nightmare.

They voted for team blue because they know that they care, for everyone, not just white billionaires.

Team blue has a lot to do, the country needed to heal from all they'd been through.

Part of that healing is writing the wrongs, removing hateful words from movies and songs.

Removing monuments to criminals who lost the civil war, we know you don't deserve our respect anymore.

People are not mascots so find a new name. No one should be disrespected so you can play a game.

But the people of Q want to keep their position, so they resist any change to their hateful traditions.

Team blue will keep up the fight. To make sure parents and kids at the border reunite, that people have a safe place to sleep at night and everyone enjoys basic human rights.

If you believe in justice for all and not just a few, and helping others is something you like to do, you should join team blue and be proud to be one of the good people too.

Printed in the United States
by Baker & Taylor Publisher Services